ONCE UPON A RHYME

IMAGINATION FOR
A NEW GENERATION

North Cheshire
Edited by Jessica Woodbridge

2004 PC

 Young**Writers**

First published in Great Britain in 2004 by:
Young Writers
Remus House
Coltsfoot Drive
Peterborough
PE2 9JX
Telephone: 01733 890066
Website: www.youngwriters.co.uk

SB ISBN 1 84460 524 8

Foreword

Young Writers was established in 1991 and has been passionately devoted to the promotion of reading and writing in children and young adults ever since. The quest continues today. Young Writers remains as committed to engendering the fostering of burgeoning poetic and literary talent as ever.

This year's Young Writers competition has proven as vibrant and dynamic as ever and we are delighted to present a showcase of the best poetry from across the UK. Each poem has been carefully selected from a wealth of *Once Upon A Rhyme* entries before ultimately being published in this, our twelfth primary school poetry series.

Once again, we have been supremely impressed by the overall high quality of the entries we have received. The imagination, energy and creativity which has gone into each young writer's entry made choosing the best poems a challenging and often difficult but ultimately hugely rewarding task - the general high standard of the work submitted amply vindicating this opportunity to bring their poetry to a larger appreciative audience.

We sincerely hope you are pleased with our final selection and that you will enjoy *Once Upon A Rhyme North Cheshire* for many years to come.

Contents

Rebecca Whitney (11)   71
Chloe O'Connor (10)   72
Josh McNulty (11)   73
Siana Redfern (10)   74
Chloe Hughes (10)   75
Joshua Harding (10)   76
Nayam Patel (11)   77
Nathan Holyoak (10)   78
Aaron Durrant (9)   79

Romiley Primary School
Katie Young (10)   80
Emma Kavanagh (10)   81
Lauren Smith (10) & Emily Roche (9)   82
Alice Rothwell (10)   83
Connie Wakefield (9)   84
Lauren Gregory (10)   85
Francesca Cassinelli (9)   86
Amy Rochford (10)   87
Emma Rheinberg (10)   88
Emily Parker (11) & Saffron Rain (9)   89
Samantha Green (9)   90
Shadia El Mokdad (10)   91
Sophie Barker (11)   92
Ben Blowers (10)   93
Jack Vanstone (11)   94
Maisie Dean (10)   95
Elizabeth Elliot (10)   96
Jessica Hadfield & Melanie Davies (11)   98
Matthew Nuttall (10)   99
Megan Hughes (8)   100
Kate Ashton-Butler (11)   101
Marcus McNulty (10)   102
Nicole Shaffi (10)   103
Rebecca Nelson (10)   104

St Bridget's RC Primary School, Warrington
Andrew Roberts (9)   105
Stuart Simm (10)   106
Daniel Mahoney (9)   107
Alicia Wright (10)   108

Alexander Hardy (10)   109
Natalie Dobbin (10)   110
Andrew Roe (10)   111
Samuel Mulholland (10)   112
Toni Armstrong (9)   113
Jordan Sutton (10)   114
Louise Mannion (9)   115

St Paul of the Cross RC Primary School, Warrington
Oliver Morrissey (9) & Connor Irving (10)   116
Danielle Drinkel & Laura Cawley (10)   117
Alex Gordon & Michael Rafferty (10)   118
Laura Wynne & Michael Pearce (10)   119
Sam O'Garra & Claire Scott (10)   120
Lucy Smith (10) & Laura Cooke-Jones (9)   121

Styal CP School
Zachary Later (10)   122
Katie Halliwell (10)   123
Molly Finnigan (9)   124
Tim Marshall (11)   125
Madeleine Smith (9)   126
Jack Holmes (9)   127
Nina Lynch (9)   128
Ollie Bayne (11)   129
Rio Tuli (9)   130
Emily Talbot (8)   131
Eleanor Jackson (9)   132
Joanna Hyde (10)   133

Warren Wood Primary School
Hatham Rahman (11)   134
Alex Ellis (10)   135
Christopher Cooney (11)   136
Katie Hicklin (11)   137
Alice Ashurst (11)   138
Rebecca Gill (10)   139
Andrew Scott (11)   140
Adam Archer (10)   141
Sam Woodall (10)   142
Nicole Bramhall (10)   143

Wilmslow Preparatory School

The Poems

All About Alice

There once was a girl called Alice
She was a princess in a palace,
She had a very huge nose
And this is how the story goes.

She picked her nose all day
She picked her nose all night,
But one day her finger got stuck
And she got a very huge fright.

She went to the hospital
To get her finger out,
But when she got there
There were no doctors about.

So poor little Alice went home
And sat in the kitchen alone,
She looked around the room
And then she saw the broom.

She soon got her finger out
With help from the broom,
And now she looks back
And remembers she was a fool.

Lois Tyler (10)
Abingdon Primary School

Snow

The skies are blue,
The ice is clear,
The nice thick crystal
And crunchy, white snow.
Looking like clear ice
Spread out on the grass.
The snow falling on rooftops
And dropping on cliffs,
As people play snowball fights
And make snowmen.

Jodie Hargreaves (8)
Abingdon Primary School

The Future

In the future,
Will hot be cold?
Will black be white?
Will light be dark?
Will high be low?

Will clever be dumb?
Will neat be scruffy?
Will good be bad?
Will friends be enemies?

Will wet be dry?
Will rough be smooth?
Will soft be hard?
Will tall be small?

What will happen
In the future?
We don't know
Because we have no choice.
Maybe we will in the future.

Robyn Coe (11)
Abingdon Primary School

Love

Love is as pink as a little girl's rosy cheeks.
Love feels like a hot, bubbly bath on a cold day.
Love tastes like strawberries.
Love smells like fresh roses.
Love sounds like a bird singing in the morning.
Love looks like your mum and dad hugging and kissing.

Helen Uren (9)
Abingdon Primary School

Excuses!

Dear Mum

Somehow stains are on the walls
Tigers have tarred the furniture
A monster turned all the water on
Horses have galloped through the living room
The Loch Ness monster has been messing in the bath
A ghost has pushed your vase off the table
A troll has been jumping on your bed and broke it
Someone put toxic waste in the fish tank
An ogre broke all the windows
A goblin took all the plants out of the ground
An alien messed my room up
I don't like this house anymore
So I'm staying with Uncle Ned for a while.

Joshua Jackson (9)
Abingdon Primary School

Snow

Snow is white, snow is wet,
Snow is fun, so let's get set.
It's like a giant blanket over the world,
It's good for sledging and snowballs hurled.

Snow wraps its fingers round the grass,
It falls from the sky like a ballerina,
It comes down in a flake,
But at night the snowmen awake . . .

Sarah Jones (9)
Abingdon Primary School

Love And Sadness

Love is the colour of blooming roses,
Love smells like fresh strawberries,
Love sounds like a puppy sleeping,
Love looks like a fluffy baby rabbit,
Love feels like a real kiss.

Sadness is the colour of an angry blue sea,
Sadness smells like out of date blackberries,
Sadness sounds like the misty rain,
Sadness looks like you have been crying,
Sadness feels like the pain inside.

Lauren Irvine (9)
Abingdon Primary School

How Funny It Would Be

How funny it would be if I was to be a tree,
Standing up high in the sky,
Waiting for birds to come and sit on me.

How funny it would be if I was to be a fish,
Swimming and swimming in the deep blue sea,
Hiding from fishermen waiting to put me on a dish.

How funny it would be if I was to be the sun,
Sitting in space, lighting up Earth
And floating around having fun.

How funny it is just to be . . . *me!*

Hannah Goodwin (10)
Abingdon Primary School

Around The Year In Twelve Months

January is boring, nothing to look forward to.
February is full of cold.
March awakens the sleeping.
April, time to eat chocolate!
May is when I work hard at school.
June is warm and full of fun.
July is time to say goodbye.
August, relax, play and holiday.
September, back to normality.
October, Christmas gets closer.
November, fire and sparkle.
December, a time for families.

Brandon Choudhory (10)
Abingdon Primary School

Dalmatian Began

For her teeth
She took the sharpness of the bladed razor,
She stole the white of the fluffy clouds,
She grabbed the smooth surface of a glass marble.

For her claws
She pinched the length of a pen,
She robbed the point of a sharp arrow,
She borrowed the sharpness of a metal knife.

For her fur
She snatched the softness of the warm quilt,
She caught the black of the coal,
She used the white of the snow.

For her growl
She took the loudness of a crying elephant,
She stole the deep sound of a loud trumpet,
She grabbed the power of an erupting volcano.

For her nose
She pinched the coldness of the cold ice,
She stole the wetness of the sea,
She borrowed the softness of a ball of wool.

Megan Worsley (10)
Abingdon Primary School

Elephant Began

For her skin
She stole the wrinkles from a screwed up paper bag
She took the sagginess from ropes
And that's how her skin was made.

For her tail
She took a bend from a snake
She stole the length from a tree trunk
And that's how her tail was made.

For her ears
She stole floppiness from the ship's sail
And that's how her ears were made.

For her trunk
She stole the length from the hosepipe
She stole the bend from the snake
And that was how her trunk was made.

Rebecca Watts (10)
Abingdon Primary School

Monkey Began

For her face
She sneaked the cheek of a street urchin
She nicked the winking of a new penny for her eyes
She stole buttons for her ears
She grabbed coal for her nose.

For her body
She grabbed the solidity of a brick wall
She sneaked her chubbiness from a jolly old man
She stole her roundness from a round teddy bear's tummy
She nicked the colour from a mudslide.

For her hands
She stole the long from breadsticks
She took the boniness from twigs
She nicked the flexibility from a worm
She grabbed the strength from Superglue.

For her tail
She stole the length from a giraffe's neck
She nicked the bend of a rubber band
She sneaked the twitch of a flea
She took the curve of the end of an umbrella.

For her feet
She stole the size of a dinner plate
She snatched ugliness from an ogre
She nicked the hairiness from a mammoth
She grabbed the flat of a pancake.

Catriona Cross (11)
Abingdon Primary School

Food, Glorious Food

Pepperami is a stick,
Covered with things that make you sick,
In a wrapper brown and green,
Makes it look big and mean.

Pizza is just the best,
Cos it's different to all the rest,
Eat it hot, eat it cold,
Eat it now before you're old.

Eggs are smelly but good to eat,
The only problem is they smell of feet,
Eat 'em boiled or eat 'em fried,
But make sure not to eat the chicks inside.

Rashers of bacon come from pigs,
They are scoffed by all the kids,
Nice and crispy, golden brown,
They can please the entire town.

Daniel Jones (11)
Abingdon Primary School

Winter Snow

Snow is fun and crunchy,
It sparkles just like the sun,
When it falls down from Heaven,
It makes me very happy.

I love snowball fights,
I get covered in soft, white snow,
People make snow angels,
They find it so much fun.

Cars are iced over,
Some engines do not start,
It wraps its fingers around the grass
And covers it with a smooth coat of frost.

Daniel Wynne (8)
Abingdon Primary School

Seasons!

Summer's hot,
You're in a knot
And you feel all sweaty.

Autumn is on its way,
The leaves are falling every day,
The trees are bare because there is cold in the air.

Winter is here,
You're full of a cold
And you need to go to someone dear and have a bit of cheer.

Spring comes every year
And when it comes it brings us cheer.

Abbie Wick (8)
Abingdon Primary School

The Pirates

The pirates have lumpy faces
Some pirates have eye patches
Some don't have them in fact they have a wooden leg
They have a sword sharper than a cheetah's tooth
They have parrots on their shoulders that can talk
Have you seen their flag yet? It's scary.

Kayleigh Muffett (8)
Abingdon Primary School

Red

Red is a beautiful Tudor rose.
Red is a spot on the end of your nose.
Red is the colour of the planet Mars.
Red is the colour of shiny cars.
Red is a yummy, crunchy apple.
Red is a blazing fireball.
Red is the tomato ketchup on my plate.
Red is a fiery sunset.
Red is the blood trickling down my cut finger.
Red is my lipstick on my lips.

Sally Urmston (8)
Banks Lane Junior School

Red

Red is a scaly, shimmering dragon.
Red is the fiery planet Mars.
Red is fresh blood.
Red is the colour of a lovely rose.
Red is a glowing, fiery sunset.
Red is a hot chilli.
Red is something dead.
Red is my sweaty forehead.
Red is a chameleon.
Red is United's kit.

Jared Phanco (8)
Banks Lane Junior School

As

As dumb as a dog - as deaf as a post,
As ugly as a pig - as horrible as burnt toast.
As slimy as a slug - as silly as a cat,
As dead as a stone - as dirty as a rat.
As warty as a witch - as plump as a toad,
As annoying as a cow lying in the middle of the road.
As sneaky as a goblin - as spooky as a castle,
As shady as a snake - or a dark coloured pastel.

Lydia Howbrook (10)
Banks Lane Junior School

As

As shiny as jewellery - as dull as rocks,
As scented as perfume - as smelly as socks.
As hard as nails - as comfy as a chair,
As small as a mouse - as big as a bear.
As squashy as a cushion - as hard as a book,
As black as a hole - as white as a duck.
As straight as a ruler - as floppy as hair,
As horrible as vegetables - as tasty as a pear.

Bethany Gaskell (9)
Banks Lane Junior School

Rhyming Opposites

As dark as the night - as bright as a light,
As heavy as a boulder - as light as a kite.
As small as a rat - as big as a cat,
As hard as wood - as soft as a hat.
As tall as a tree - as short as a bee,
As strong as a giant - as weak as a flea.
As clean as a sock - as dirty as a rock,
As dry as a desert - as wet as a dock.

Ryan Williams (9)
Banks Lane Junior School

As

As shiny as an apple - as dirty as mud,
As quiet as a mouse - as loud as a thud.
As strong as a bull - as weak as a mouse,
As soft as a pillow - as hard as a house.
As tall as a tree - as small as a rat,
As fat as a sumo - as flat as a mat.
As wet as the sea - as dry as a pea,
As happy as a hyena - as sad as me.

Thomas Derbyshire (9)
Banks Lane Junior School

Opposites

As wet as the sea - as dry as a snake,
As small as a mouse - as large as a rake.
As cool as a fridge - as hot as the sun,
As yukky as sprouts - as yummy as a bun.
As shiny as gold - as rusty as a gate,
As nasty as my enemy - as kind as my mate.
As bright as light - as dull as the dark,
As boring as lines - as fun as the park!

Matthew Hopkins & Melissa Bradley (10)
Banks Lane Junior School

As

As red as a rose - as wet as water,
As bright as a ball - as dull as a daughter.
As clear as crystal - as frozen as fingers,
As compact as a car - as significant as singers.
As solid as a seat - as fragile as a flower,
As small as a snail - as tall as a tower.
As dainty as a daisy - as hungry as a horse,
As flopsy as a fairy - as spicy as a sauce.

Shelby Whyatt (9)
Banks Lane Junior School

Similes Special

As slow as a slug - as fast as a cheetah,
As short as a pen - as long as a metre.
As shallow as a puddle - as deep as the sea,
As quiet as a mouse - as busy as a bee.
As clever as a book - as thick as a board,
As blunt as a pencil - as sharp as a sword.
As spiky as a hedgehog - as furry as a fox,
As exciting as a fair - as boring as a box.

Lauren Taylor-Burke (10) & Thomas Palfreyman (9)
Banks Lane Junior School

Opposites

As dark as a castle - as bright as a pastel,
As good as silence - as bad as hassle.
As visible as a post - as invisible as a ghost,
As cold as winter - as hot as toast.
As spotty as a dog - as slimy as a frog,
As moving as a cheetah - as still as a log.
As dainty as a lady - as big as a man,
As clean as a plate - as rusty as a pan.

Daniel Bowman (10) & Chantelle Francis (9)
Banks Lane Junior School

Snow

As the icy, white body arises,
Her fingers sprinkle snow on mountain tops,
As her dress sweeps the ground,
It leaves behind snowy paths like snail trails.
A sudden breeze quickens her steps,
Each tree and shrub waves as she passes,
The children bow down to her kindness.
She thinks she's a snake,
Sticking her white venom in everything that comes in her way,
She steps on a red rose
And ice trickles down.
Anger is forming in her eyes,
As her mouth opens she lets out a scream.
A blizzard flies out as if it were a rocket,
She becomes more and more angry,
Until she starts to choke.
She chokes and chokes,
Out comes the sun,
Its shining glow cutting her like knives,
Until it melts her completely.
Next year she will come again
And the next and the next.

Emma Bowers (11)
Banks Lane Junior School

Snow

A big, giant blanket,
A crunchy, white crisp,
The path lay ahead of me,
A long, winding whip.
Softly and gently
It falls like sugar.
As if the clouds were falling,
Piece by piece
Little bits fell to the ground.
The trees were covered,
As if wearing white cloaks.
Your feet sink with a crunch, crunch,
In the wonderful, magical, powdery
Snow!

Jordan Turner (11)
Banks Lane Junior School

Snow

Snowflakes falling like feathers,
Lighter than the air itself,
The crunching sound beneath our feet,
Louder than the autumn leaves,
But quieter than the shout of man.
The glistening white, reflecting the sun,
Keeping grass warm
And dressing the trees.

Though it is cold,
Its spirit is warm.
With snowmen made
And snowball fights,
Nothing can beat it,
Not even summer sand.

Ken Skarratt (10)
Banks Lane Junior School

Snow

Sparkling glitter as white as a sheep,
Fluffy and magical to touch,
Like a cloud, but ice-cold,
Spread over the hard ground,
Bringing enchantment to the people.
Animals pad their tiny feet in my soft snow,
The moon steps out and covers the land with silver,
Through the night I sleep peacefully,
I dream of snow.
When I wake I dance across the unmarked snow,
Suddenly flakes fall from the sky,
Sprinkling me with delight.

Emma Stewart (11)
Banks Lane Junior School

A Snowy Day

I opened the door
It was snowy and cold
Sweet and exciting
The branches of the tree
Were dripping with glistening snow.
It sparkled like diamonds
And the world looked like a very special place.

Callum McEvoy (10)
Banks Lane Junior School

Through The Window

I see life . . .
When I am older I run and jump
When I am older I will go silly
When I am older I will shout at people
And they will jump in fright
When I am older I will spend my savings
On beer and brandy and say it wasn't me!
When I am older I will say we've no money for shopping
When I am older I will say I'm going to bed!
Life!
Through the window.

Michael Rathbone (9)
Golborne CP School

Through The Window

I see that . . .
She's a pencil that's always working hard
She's an early morning sun
She's a light daffodil rising quicker than ever
She's the light yellow sun because she's happy with glory
She's light blue - yes, that's her colour
She's a cheetah running around
She is my best friend.

Gemma Ratcliffe (8)
Golborne CP School

My Day

Rise and shine
Breakfast time
Get dressed
In your best
Talk
While you walk
Go in
Put your chewy in the bin
Do your maths
Really fast.

Abbie Egerton (8)
Golborne CP School

My Day

Morning dawns
Everyone yawns
I fuss
Then I miss the bus
In the playground
My head is going round
Get home
Use the phone
Eat a pie
Then tell a lie
First I walk
Then I talk
Count sheep
Then go to sleep.

Mica Carlon (8)
Golborne CP School

When I Was A Child

When I was a child I hoped
When I was a child I cried
When I was a child I ran
When I was a child I grew
When I was a child I talked
When I was a child I clapped
When I was a child I was me
When I was a child I smiled.

Lorna Smith (9)
Golborne CP School

My Best Friend's Wedding

We all rush around combing her hair
And lots of make-up goes everywhere
And all of the dresses pink and blue
Plus the special bride's dress too
Gets wrecked and ruined, ripped in two!

We get into the car with the bride
We have an argument over who will drive
Then the neighbour's dog
Hops in for a ride.

We push, shove into a tree
Then we have to let the dog outside for a wee
It decides to run off and go for a play
We're going to get there sometime today.

We finally get there in a state
We were very nearly late
The bride gets her dress stuck in the door
Then it ripped and tore.

We go inside the church so bright
Then the bride realizes her dress is no longer white
'Oh no!' she says, 'I just remembered my wedding isn't today
It's on Saturday!'

Kate Stafford (10)
Gorsey Bank Primary School

The Gnome

In the land of Spittle
Where the cows are brittle
There lives a little gnome
He went to the pub
And sang for his grub

He went to the shed
And bumped his head
His eyes went fuzzy
He fell to the ground
And lost all sound

In the morning
When it was dawning
He woke with a sore head
Was it the beer or was it the bump?
He looked in the mirror and saw a large lump

He went to the pharmacist for a lotion or potion
To relieve him of his sore head
But after a few days all he had was . . .
A terrible bowel motion!

Rory Fisher (11)
Gorsey Bank Primary School

Guess Who?

Try and guess who.
I'll give you a clue.
With her long, floppy ears
And her long whiskers too,
Her cuddly, long fur
And her dark brown eyes.
Now try and guess who.

Anna Chatfield (11)
Gorsey Bank Primary School

Snow

As I went to bed all snug and warm,
I heard a pattering sound out on the lawn.
I looked out the window and what did I see?
A blanket of white snow surrounding me!

I ran downstairs and put on my shoes,
This was a chance I could not lose.
I opened the door and in the night,
I felt the crisp snow, what a delight!

As I played around in the snow,
I wondered if I was first to know
About this winter wonderland,
I wanted it to stay, as I'd hoped and planned.

In the morning the snow had gone
And then I knew I was the only one,
Who'd been out in the snow to play.
I hope it comes another day!

Emma Partington (10)
Gorsey Bank Primary School

My Planet

My planet is,
All the colours of the rainbow,
Blue, pink, white and green.
My planet has animals with horns,
Animals big, animals small,
Animals short, animals tall.

My planet has,
Plants as big as towers,
Plants as small as a mouse,
Flowers that glow,
Flowers that are bright,
Pink, purple, yellow and white.
My planet is special, fantastic and fun,
My planet is
The best in the world,
The best in space,
The best in the whole universe.

On my planet,
There would be no fighting,
No such thing as war.
Everyone would own their own front door,
People would not hurt animals anymore.
No one would be hungry,
Everyone would have a friend,
This would be my planet.

Isobelle Duggan (11)
Gorsey Bank Primary School

The Town Is Burning

The sun is shining,
The wood is burning,
The town is in danger.
Everyone is panicking,
The fire is spreading,
Buildings are falling.

The fire engine is rushing,
The people are waiting,
The town is saved.
The people are relieved,
The water has saved everyone,
The fire has stopped.

Sami Watson (10)
Gorsey Bank Primary School

Butterflies

How the different colours are made,
How the butterflies fly,
How big they are is amazing,
In the big, blue sky.

I think they are beautiful,
In every single way,
With all the trees,
I love it that they stay.

The way they fly is magnificent,
Just looking at them makes me smile,
It's like my family,
I haven't seen one in a while.

I think about them all the time,
I can't concentrate,
Thank you for butterflies,
They're like my mate.

Kirsty Rhodes (10)
Gorsey Bank Primary School

Holiday Season

It's holiday season,
There's only one reason,
It's sun, sea, sand,
On only, one land,
The silver backed water,
Hip, hip, hurrah, it's holiday season.

A fly in the air,
It's such a scare,
Is it cold?
It's sold
To the man in the red,
Hip, hip, hurrah, it's holiday season.

It's off to the pool,
It's really cool,
I am wet, also my pet,
Use suntan lotion,
There's so much motion,
Hip, hip, hurrah, it's holiday season.

Jasmine Redwood (10)
Gorsey Bank Primary School

My Butterfly

My butterfly is so beautiful,
With her rainbow-coloured wings.
I wish I could watch her every day,
Just fluttering in the breeze.
When summer comes and flowers bloom,
The sun will sparkle on her wings.
Oh why, oh why can't I fly,
Over the pretty flowers.
My butterfly's so beautiful,
In every single way.

Katy Taylor (10)
Gorsey Bank Primary School

My Food Poem

I like jelly,
I like rice,
I like curry,
They are nice.

I like ice cream,
I like cake,
I like chips,
Pizzas that you can make.

I like marshmallows,
I like toast,
I like chicken
That you can roast.

I like chocolate,
I like cheese,
I like oranges,
But I don't like peas.

Matthew Nicholls (10)
Gorsey Bank Primary School

Teachers' Pets

My teacher, Miss Drake,
Has a snake.
It's a python
And it's called Minathonnon.
But it's not a normal snake,
Or why is it kept by Miss Drake?
It has eyes of an owl,
It has a fox's scowl,
The head of a sow
And the tongue of a cow.

My teacher, Mr Higgs,
Keeps pigs.
One's called Fatty,
One's called Hatty,
But these aren't normal pigs,
Or why would they be kept by Mr Higgs?
They have legs of cats,
Tails of rats,
Bodies of warthogs
And heads of dogs.

Sarah Bowen (10)
Gorsey Bank Primary School

What Teachers Look Like

Mrs Peate,
Is always looking neat.

Miss Holly,
Wore a dress that made her look like Miss Polly.

Mr Goulding's glasses
Are always folding.

Miss Mayers,
Always wears layers.

Mr Brown,
Always has a frown.

Mr Smith,
With a quiff.

Victoria Brickhill (10)
Gorsey Bank Primary School

School!

Maths is a sin,
An ordinary din,
The worst is the teacher,
A weird and vulgar creature,
That's what I've named the teacher!

Science is a chore,
An everyday bore,
What's evaporation?
I don't call that education.

Literacy is a disaster,
A time for much laughter,
Spellings once a week,
For the answer I seek.

Zoë Perera (11)
Gorsey Bank Primary School

My Pet!

My pet would have to be small,
Cute, furry, but not tall.
I want to be able to dress up my pet
And never have to take it to the vet.
I want my pet not to bite,
But to be strong with might.
I want my pet to help every day
And come to school with me all the way.
My pet would always listen to me,
Especially when there's an emergency.
My pet would change into other things
And maybe even have wings.
I don't want my pet to be very smelly
And definitely not to have a big belly.
I don't want my pet to run away,
I want it to be home safe and stay.

Rebecca Chin (10)
Gorsey Bank Primary School

My Beach

My sand is gold sand,
Glittery, shiny and clean,
Looking new, brand new, new for the day.

My sea is a turquoise sea,
Seaweed spread all around,
Looking new, brand new, new for the day.

My sand is gold sand,
Glittery, shiny and clean,
Looking new, brand new, new for the day.

Katherine Hassell (10)
Gorsey Bank Primary School

Another World

Another world under the sea
To the gate it needs a key
Which leads to another sea!

Another world under the sea
Which has a big banana tree!
The sea monkeys are going to flee
And going to have a cup of tea.

Another world under the sea
The sea monkeys are waiting to plea
To the god under the sea.

Another world under the sea
The bumblebees are coming to look at me!
I have a friend, his name is Lee
He lives next door to me under the sea!

Another world under the sea
To the gate it needs a key
Which leads to another sea!

Oh, it is the place to be!

Jessica Legge (10)
Gorsey Bank Primary School

Decotion

Years ago, under the ocean,
There was a land called Decotion.
This land was inhabited by trillions of fish,
All the kinds, anything you wish.
And in the middle there was a castle,
Ruled by the fish king, great Carastle.
One day, the prince of West Decotion,
Set a battle in the ocean.
Great Carastle was no more,
The prince of West Decotion won the war.

But nowadays, under the ocean,
There is no such thing as the land Decotion.

Danielle Harrison (11)
Gorsey Bank Primary School

The Battle Of The Three-Headed Cats And The Ten-Eyed Rats

The battle has started,
Who will win?
The three-headed cats
Or the ten-eyed rats.

No one knows,
Not one single soul.
Who will win,
Cats or rats?

It's been three years
And the battle's still going.
Neither have won,
Cats or rats.

It's been four years
And there's blood everywhere.
The battle is done,
The evil three-headed cats have won.

Beth Morris (11)
Gorsey Bank Primary School

A Wizard's Meal

A sugared rat and a peppered cat
With an eye of hog and leg of frog
And that's only for starters

Eyeball stew and a dog with flu
Head of lizard and snow from blizzard
And that's for the main course

Carrot cake that he can make
A lamb's heart and a blood tart
And that's a wizard's meal.

Charlie Entwistle (11)
Gorsey Bank Primary School

How Do You Imagine?

How do you imagine?
Close your eyes and think, what do you see?
Are you a knight in shining armour,
About to defeat a fire-breathing dragon?

How do you imagine?
Imagine, imagine, imagine, what do you see?
Is the world at your feet?
Are you the queen?

How do you imagine?
Close your eyes, close your eyes, what do you see?
Are you in China,
Drinking a cup of tea?

How do you imagine?
Think, think, close your eyes and think.
What do you see?
Are you a polar bear hunting fish?

How do you imagine?
Close your eyes and think, what do you see?
Are you an Egyptian pharaoh,
Admiring your father's pyramid?

How do you imagine?
Imagine, imagine, imagine, what do you see?
Are you a newborn baby,
Opening her eyes for the first time?

How do you imagine?
Think, think, close your eyes and think,
What do you see?
Are you a lioness proudly looking after her cubs?

Now you know how to imagine,
Where would you like to be?
Imagine, imagine, imagine,
Close your eyes, what do you see?

Jade Armstrong (10)
Gorsey Bank Primary School

Swogghopper

I was cruising space,
When I found
A small baby creature,
Furry and round,
With bright pink eyes
And a sharp blue tail,
Wandering legs
And as small as a quail.

I picked it up
And stroked its fur,
Then to my surprise
It began to purr.
Its eyes were dreamy
And its legs fat,
But then another surprise,
It opened its wings
Just like a bat.

It curled up close
And had a sleep,
It was so quiet,
Not one peep.
I named him Swogghopper
And he lived almost forever,
I will never sell him,
Never, never.

Victoria Wilford (10)
Gorsey Bank Primary School

The Night

At night the vampires strike.
They come to take your blood and all.
It's not something I like.
They come one by one, big and tall.

They wrap their mouth around your neck
And take a little sip,
Just trying it out.
Then if they like it, they kill you with a nip!
Eventually, when finished, they're off while you're in doubt.

And then they strike again and again.
Evil as ever.
Never ceasing to gain.
So what I say is never, never become a vampire.
Never!

Jonathan Stubbs (10)
Gorsey Bank Primary School

Scary Poem

Once upon a time
There was a ghost called Ben
And three little people
Called Mum, Luke and Gwen.
They went for a walk
And met up with ghostly Ben
The ghost said, 'We will meet later
In the park near the foxes' den.'
Mum said, 'Let's have lunch first.'
They had a McDonald's near Big Ben
Then it was time to go.
On the way they saw a wren
Singing by the foxes' den
Out popped ghostly Ben
'Hi,' said Ben
To Mum, Luke and Gwen,
'Please follow me
To my ghostly den.'
They followed Ben
Round the park to his ghostly den
What a surprise they got
For today was ghostly Ben's
Birthday party bash.
A birthday cake and candles ten
And balloons and streamers
Presents from Mum, Luke and Gwen
What a party for ghostly Ben.
Now it was time to sing
'Happy birthday ghostly Ben
Happy birthday ten today.'

Ben Robinson (10)
Gorsey Bank Primary School

The Other Planet From Nowhere

As the rocket flew through the night
Some hours later the captain took fright
He looked out the window that looked like a bowl
And he fainted at the sight of a giant black hole!

Whizzing and shirling
The rocket was twirling
The hole had sucked the spacecraft in
And squashed the crew really thin.

The next thing they noticed they were in a weird place
And there was an alien with a head like a briefcase
The astronauts looked round at shapes like an egg
That's when the alien fell over and broke his leg.

He went off hobbling to his home
That looked to the world like the Millennium Dome
In the centre of the planet an enormous city thrives
With lots of strange creatures living busy lives.

The astronauts walked over to a cool looking pod
They asked for a room from a weird looking bod
The life there seemed good and the food was just right
So they decided to stay for at least a fortnight.

Richard Bull (11)
Gorsey Bank Primary School

Trouble

T empers rising quickly
R obbed from the corner shop
'O i!' shouted a policeman
U nder the fences, over the wall
B ehind the bins
L et's get him
E scape quickly.

Connair Tipler (8)
Oakenclough School

Chips

C runchy, crispy, fat
H ot and lovely
I mpossible to leave
P erfect
S alty, go with fish.

Anthony O'Connor (9)
Oakenclough School

Penguin

P ointing feet
E xciting ice
N oisy, whistling chicks
G reedy females
U nder ice looking for fish
I cy, soft snow
N oisy birds on the ice.

Jenny Marcinkiw (8)
Oakenclough School

Brother

B rilliant brother
R ules the house
O ut every day
T op brother
H elps around the house
E xcellent footballer
R eally cool friend.

Rebecca Hayes, Rebecca Norbury (8) & Jade Durrant (7)
Oakenclough School

Dog Attack

On last year's Hallowe'en,
A dog bit Mr Bean,
Unhinged by this attack,
Mr Bean bit it back.

He bit it with his molars
And tore it with his canines
And crunched it with his fangs
And then bit him with all of his teeth.

On last year's Halloween,
A dog bit Mr Bean,
And now Mr Bean feels good,
But the dog is in a puddle of blood.

Abbey Pochec (8)
Oakenclough School

Fairy

F airy dust shimmering in the moonlight.
A ll around an enchanted wood.
I mps and elves skipping in the fairy dance.
R ound and round the sprites sing.
Y ellow waterfall rushing down.

Georgina Crehan
Oakenclough School

Thunder

T umbling rain
H iding in your house
U ntil it stops
N oisy thunder
D eafening our ears
E verywhere is dark
R eally scary.

Thomas Fielding (9)
Oakenclough School

Fire & Cash

F laming hot
I t is dangerous
R ed-hot
E vil flames.

C ostly cars
A shiny coin
S pending money
H elping.

Daniel Ward (9)
Oakenclough School

Love Your Dog

I love dogs:
Their bark
Their shout
Their fur is as soft as a velvet blanket
Their eyes are shiny like marbles
Why not look into your dog's eyes
And say what you think of your cute little dog
Don't be mean to your dog
Love it like a proper owner would.

Jade Bell (10)
Oakenclough School

The Fairground

People screaming
Rides breaking down
Children eating big, pink clouds
Getting it everywhere
Smothering it on their faces
Granny's walking miles behind
Dad's sitting reading the paper
People clutching their stomachs
Going red in their faces
Fairground workers running round with buckets
People walking in and out
Children moaning
Babies squealing
Tomato sauce everywhere
Security guards looking for trouble
Cafés full
Time to go.

Rebecca Whelan (11)
Oakenclough School

The Rose

In the hot sun, the grass rocks from side to side like a wonky straw,
With the one single little rose.
She looked like a lonely schoolgirl,
Her leaves reach out for help.
Her petals fall off with anger and sadness,
Her stalk's ready to snap.
Giant hands reach towards her like two pairs of scissors.
They pick her little, bendy stalk and put her into a strange vase
With lots of other red roses.
She felt so happy there and her petals grew beautiful
With the colour of a red rose lipstick.
Her stalk grew straight, as straight as a ruler.
Her leaves still reach, reach out for help,
But only to play with her new friends.

Rebecca Whitney (11)
Oakenclough School

The Landing

Storm and black clouds suddenly break with blue sky,
Salty waves push against the pier.
High seagulls look down,
The blowing sails make the boats rock from side to side.
Men row hard and one shouts into the wind.
Frightened passengers want to get onto the pier,
Waiting friends will be glad to see them.

Chloe O'Connor (10)
Oakenclough School

A Snake Poem

Green, soft, wiggly snake
Just as fast as a cheetah
Wiggling through the grass
Watching its prey
Like a lion after a zebra.

Josh McNulty (11)
Oakenclough School

Snow

The snow is white
And it is as cold as an iceberg.
The snow is rough.
The snow is beautiful.
The snow only comes in the winter.
The snow looks like a polar bear
And a fluffy, white rabbit.

Siana Redfern (10)
Oakenclough School

Tree Poem

The leaves fall off in autumn,
The leaves are yellow, orange and red like a fire,
The branches go like old grannies' hands
And in summer they come back.

Chloe Hughes (10)
Oakenclough School

Nature

The trees are bright green and stand tall.
The leaves fall off in winter and turn into flowers.
Then in summer the flowers die and change into fruit.
When the fruit is sweet, people gather it and eat it.
But in winter, trees go to sleep
And in summer the trees come alive to hear the birds sing.

Joshua Harding (10)
Oakenclough School

Summer

As hot as the Sahara Desert
Cool waterfights
Ice-cold drinks
Like freezing icicles
The burning sun
Melting ice creams
Flying waterbombs
People buying chilly ice buckets
People praying for frosty snow
People sunbathing in the boiling heat
Suntan lotion getting sold like hot cakes
People on the grass
Looking forward to a tan
Chocolate melting
As fast as a tiger catching its prey
As the warmth gets closer to -
Autumn.

Nayam Patel (11)
Oakenclough School

The Bridge

A bridge stands low, a bridge stands high
Over a river, over a road
Cars go fast, boats go slow
So many things under a bridge
Too many traffic jams
Too many boats passing by
Causing car crashes
Boat crashes too
So many things under a bridge
All by petrol nothing else.

Nathan Holyoak (10)
Oakenclough School

Mum

M um in charge of the house
U sually she washes my undies
M um makes lovely chips.

Aaron Durrant (9)
Oakenclough School

Snow Is Here

On a winter's night cold as ice,
You may think it will be nice.
You know Jack Frost is here,
Now he is here you have no fear.

Children playing in the night,
When the stars are shining bright.
Now winter is here children laugh with cheer
And adults are drinking lots of beer.

Katie Young (10)
Romiley Primary School

Golden

Shining brightly, now the sun
Ships the day having golden fun;
This way and that, she peeps and spies
Golden clouds on bright blue skies;
Two by two the doors unlatch
Her smile beams as eggs hatch;
Lies in her bed, like a log
With dreams of gold sleeps the hedgehog;
From their sunny hat the yellow breast sleep
Of swans in a goldy-feathered keep;
A spring rat goes scampering by
With golden paws and a golden pie;
A sea horse in the water gleams
With golden beads in golden streams.

Emma Kavanagh (10)
Romiley Primary School

Ice Dragon

How far had he flown?
It is not known.
How was he made?
From ice they said.

He flew up higher and higher,
Blowing out icy fire.
Icicle scales
And teeth like nails.

He made a noise like a lion,
His fire becoming as hot as an iron.
His tail was flicking round and round,
The wind blowing his icicles to the ground.

The sun came out
And suddenly came a rainy drought,
A puddle formed on the floor,
Here the ice dragon lay before.

Lauren Smith (10) & Emily Roche (9)
Romiley Primary School

The Sea

As lightning strikes,
He faces his fear, as a blue knight.
He chews at the shore
And washes land raw.
Night becomes day,
He flows his own way.

He calls out to the world,
In his silent voice,
Boats drift out,
As if they were his toys.
He owns life, down beneath,
He breaks rocks with his blue teeth.

He gives the world a bluish gleam,
He sits day by day, eager and keen.
The gentle waves tickle our toes,
He spreads across to where it's cold.

Alice Rothwell (10)
Romiley Primary School

Snowflakes

Snowflakes crisp and clear
Glittering at the pier.

Snowflakes fall at midnight
In the shimmering moonlight.

Snowflakes as cold as ice,
But they're all so nice as nice.

Snowflakes fall from the sky,
But all of a sudden they drop and die.

Snowflakes.

Connie Wakefield (9)
Romiley Primary School

Snowball

In the soft, snowy street
At every stride snow sticks to your feet
The dog is barking as loud as light
The snow is sparkling snowy and bright.

As the very fierce rain came down from the drain
At every footstep breaks a brittle pain
As it started to snow, the rooftops began to glow.

As we build something white, round and tall
It is not a snowman, but a snowball.

Lauren Gregory (10)
Romiley Primary School

Snowball

The cold, icy snow covers the street,
And every step brings snow to your feet.
A blanket of white, cold stuff all soft and thick,
You could move it with just one gentle kick.
As we build something white, round and tall,
It's not a snowman, but a snowball!

Francesca Cassinelli (9)
Romiley Primary School

After School

School is finished,
Children gone,
A flock of birds go,
Squawking on.

A packet of crisps,
A biscuit or two,
Whatever they can find,
Just so they don't catch the flu.

Amy Rochford (10)
Romiley Primary School

Ghost Girl

Down below the creaking trees,
A voice is calling, 'Please, please.'

A small, ghostly girl,
Stands as white as a pearl.

Her clothes are rags,
They look like torn bags.

With a voice like a frog,
She sits crying on a log.

When people look and scream,
She disappears, nowhere to be seen.

The ancient forest can set a scene,
For her to let off a misty gleam.

When I went there, saw her face, clothes and hair,
She didn't half give me a scare!

Emma Rheinberg (10)
Romiley Primary School

Story Book

Once upon a time,
As story books will say,
Where fairy tales were mixed,
In a castle far away.

With princesses in dungeons,
And dragons on the throne,
Out in the castle gardens,
Came a muffled moan.

Three wee pigs in a flurry,
The wolf had puffed and blown,
Three blind mice truly lost this time,
Can't find their own way home.

Cinderella lost her special shoe,
Mislaid it at the ball,
Two ugly sisters don't even care,
They're shopping at the mall!

Snow White has finally been kissed,
Awoken with a smile,
Seven dwarves dance and sing along,
All are happy . . . for a while!

Emily Parker (11) & Saffron Rain (9)
Romiley Primary School

Snowball Poem

The cold, snowy street,
Will always tickle your feet,
At every step of the way,
You might just have to play,
A white, soft blanket covers the walkway,
Every minute of a winter day.

You play, you have fun, it never stops,
You'll love it, just trust me lots,
We build snowmen and snowgirls,
We build snowgirls with white, shining pearls,
We have fun building them tall,
Eventually we put them all together
And make a giant snowball!

Samantha Green (9)
Romiley Primary School

Christmas

Cold candyfloss covers the street,
Every stride brings snow to your feet,
As children play in the park,
People make a snowy mark,
As snowballs roll down the hill,
They act like flour in a mill.

Christmas comes and Christmas goes,
Fires keep warm, cold fingers and toes,
Santa Claus soars away,
Rudolf, Prancer, pulling his sleigh,
Children play with toys and kites,
While mums and dads take down the lights.

When the snowmen melt and the ice goes away,
Villagers wait for another snowy day,
Christmas cards are gathered up,
Children play with their Christmas pup,
The new term begins with a different sir,
Christmas forgotten for another year.

Shadia El Mokdad (10)
Romiley Primary School

The Writer Of This Poem

(Based on 'The Writer Of This Poem' by Roger McGough)

The writer of this poem
Is taller than a tree
As keen as the North Wind
As handsome as can be

As bold as a boxing glove
As sharp as a nib
As strong as scaffolding
As tricky as a fib

As smooth as an ice lolly
As quick as a lick
As clean as a chemist's shop
As clever as a tick

The writer of this poem
Never ceases to amaze
He's one in a million billion
(Or so the poem says!)

Sophie Barker (11)
Romiley Primary School

The Ghost Knight

The war is over, the soldiers gone,
But the ghost of a knight lingers on.
As the daylight fades, as the destruction ends,
As the night goes on and the dark descends,
He stands on the battlefield as clear as glass
And tramples down the dew-dropped grass.

The war is successful, the war fellow's gone,
But the ghost of a knight, all alone,
Puts his sword in his belt and walks about,
(As the knight walks on and the stars come out)
Between the bodies - aglow in the gloom,
It's the light of a torch demanding doom.

The castle is a ruin, the enemy fled,
But the ghost of a knight, long time dead,
As the moon comes up and the first owls glide,
Puts his armour to one side,
In the moonlit war ground, shadow free,
He stands on duty with a mangled knee.

The year is forgotten - kings forgot -
But the ghost of a knight lingers yet,
As the night creeps up to the edge of day,
As he wishes his troubles away;
Mounts his horse as clear as ice,
And says the war is over, peace is nice,
He utters the words that no one hears
Heel to horse and disappears.

Ben Blowers (10)
Romiley Primary School

The Abandoned Mill

The silent mill sits in the darkness
He has no will, no will, no way
He thinks to himself, 'My owner will pay
For his crime on that terrible, terrible day.

He left me here, abandoned, alone
My cogs all creak and groan
I'm not cared about anymore
He doesn't care that I'm old and poor.

As I said, I'm all alone
As my stomach starts to moan
As the day draws in and darkness is near
The sun beams out, looks strangely queer.

It reminds me of his crime that day
Burning brightness in that dreadful May
He set me on fire
That little liar
I'm not a denyer,
He set me on *fire.'*

Jack Vanstone (11)
Romiley Primary School

Baking

We're going to bake, so we'll work as a team,
Get butter and sugar and start to cream,
Add a bit of flour
And turn the spoon with power,
If needed, add baking powder,
We're all excited but not getting louder,
Measure some milk if the dough's too hard,
But definitely don't use lard,
Roll it with a rolling pin,
Make shapes with a tin,
Take them to the heater,
When they're done decorate them neater,
Put them on a plate,
Now need to wait,
So gobble them all up!

Maisie Dean (10)
Romiley Primary School

The Dark Night Sky And The Moon

The glittering moon shines on me,
Like a sparkling diamond,
While I'm eating my tea.
It comes out in the night,
It shines, it's bright and it's light!

The man on the moon,
Is eating a yoghurt with a spoon.
It's mysterious, it's light,
And it comes out at night!

When the sky is dark,
The moon shines on the park.
It comes out at night,
When the sky is not light!

Elizabeth Elliot (10)
Romiley Primary School

Impossible People

If weekdays were people . . . what kind of people would they be?

Miss Terious Monday
When I'm warm, like a hand in a glove
The atmosphere changes from kind to unloved,
A creepy shadow that lurks in the dusk
It's Miss Terious Monday - *never* give her your trust!

Tiffany Tuesday
She's the type of girl we all should meet
Pretty, attractive, like honey, she's sweet,
With an intelligent mind and glamorous smile
She's Tiffany Tuesday - you can see her from a mile.

Mr Wicked Wednesday
He laughs like a volcano, *any* time he could erupt
He's evil and a villain, a real wicked crook,
When he's out at night, the lights start to dim
He's Mr Wicked Wednesday - I *wouldn't* mess with him!

Theo Thunder Thursday
He's like a monster, a fire-breathing dragon
If you should meet, it may be Armageddon,
He's like a mist that appears here and there
He's Theo Thunder Thursday - *never* has been fair.

Freda Freaky Friday
She's just plain weird and totally nuts
She puts the Fry in Friday without any buts,
She's bouncy and bubbly like a ball
She's Freda Freaky Friday - just give her a call.

Simple Simon Saturday
He's dreary, questioning, like an unfinished book
He's clumsy, dull and has extremely bad luck,
He's easier than pie, but a really geeky guy
He's Simple Simon Saturday - *please* give him a try.

Spooky Sasha Sunday
Scarier than a haunted house
She's like a tiger ready to pounce,
She smells and looks worse than mouldy bread
She's Spooky Sasha Sunday - *perhaps* she's *dead!*

Jessica Hadfield & Melanie Davies (11)
Romiley Primary School

The Sale Sharks Coach

The dressing room closed, players gone,
The Sale Sharks coach still plays on,
As the day has passed,
Dark comes so fast,
He stands outside on the pitch,
Kicking balls out of the ditch.

The doors are shut, the floodlights are on,
But the Sale Sharks coach still plays on,
He puts his boots on whilst kicking the ball,
All the friends in his head give him their all,
He sits outside the dressing room,
As he puts his head down in doom.

He remembers the sounds of when he held the ball,
Hearing the fans calling, 'Paul, Paul, Paul,'
But those days are gone,
Yet the memory lingers on,
When the players win, they are so glad,
Why then does the coach feel really sad?

Matthew Nuttall (10)
Romiley Primary School

The Honey Bear

Honey bears, honey bears,
There they go,
Running to where the river flows.
Down the river, up the hill,
Won't waste time, no time to stand still.
At last they meet their destiny,
The world's largest honey tree!

Megan Hughes (8)
Romiley Primary School

The Mermaid

She never seemed to question
She never did ask why
She only turned her face away
And looked up at the sky

Her face was pale and pretty
Her hair it was so red
Some called her a ghost
Who had risen from the dead

She stood upon the seashore
As the sun began to die
Until the other mermaids came
She didn't ask them why

For inside she was a mermaid
Who ran to see the sun's burn
And when she was upon the sand
To the sea she could not return

She stepped right off the seashore
She stepped right off the land
She took another mermaid's arm
She left the beach's sand

Now she was with her people
She'd left behind her stress
She went down underneath the sea
The mermaid princess.

Kate Ashton-Butler (11)
Romiley Primary School

The Goalkeeper Ghost

Dressing rooms closed, players gone,
But the goalkeeper ghost still plays on,
As the daylight fades and the daytime ends,
As the night draws in and the dark descends,
He stands outside the dressing room door,
Waiting for the crowd to roar.

In the chill of the night, the floodlights are on,
As the goalkeeper ghost still plays on,
Gloves are on, he's ready to go,
Picks up the ball and takes a long throw,
His imaginary friend joins in the game,
As the crowd shout Ruud Van Nistelrooy's name.

The pitch is bare, the players have fled,
As he says hello to Fred the Red,
As the moon comes up and the coach arrives,
He puts on his coat and steps inside,
On his way home, another great game,
He put the opposition to shame.

As the night creeps in at the end of the day,
The goalkeeper ghost puts his kit away,
Another game played, another clean sheet,
This is a keeper I'd love to meet,
He utters the words that no one hears,
Picks up his boot bag and disappears.

Marcus McNulty (10)
Romiley Primary School

Rats Away

Scuttling claws from the underground,
Sewage piled up into a mound.

A pointy nose, small and pink,
It scuttles past you and gives you a wink.

Hearing scuttling in your flat,
It's bigger than a mouse, it's got to be a rat.

Rats eat whatever they find,
They're not very nice, so don't think they're kind.

All rats like to have a name,
They're all different, but not the same.

Rotten food gets thrown down there,
Don't go down there, so best beware!

Nicole Shaffi (10)
Romiley Primary School

The Snowman

Here I am in the snow,
Wondering where on earth to go.
But most of the snow has disappeared,
What am I supposed to do here?

The kids don't play outside anymore,
Their toes are numb and their fingers are sore.
So here I am with nothing to do,
But the school kids inside are probably bored too!

Well, the ice has come, I'm nearly gone,
The odds of me staying here are one million to one.
See you family, see you guys,
When I come back next year, you'll be in for a surprise.

Rebecca Nelson (10)
Romiley Primary School

Football

'Ohh, ref it's a foul over here'
He shoots, what a goal,
Into the back of the net,
He gets a goal from a foul!
Beckham was fouled.

'Pass, no not to them Giggs'
Fans are shouting,
'Come on England,'
It's 5-1 to England
In the dying seconds.

Germany are losing,
The ball goes in the air,
Just missed,
The whistle is blown,
England winds 5-1.

Andrew Roberts (9)
St Bridget's RC Primary School, Warrington

Somewhere In The World Today

Somewhere in the world today . . .
A troop of sabre-toothed tigers
Are cornering a lazy mammoth
In the freezing Ice Age.

A group of vicious cats purring noisily,
In a dark, gloomy, smelly alleyway.
A herd of frantic pigs are drinking water
Greedily on the deserted farm.

Stuart Simm (10)
St Bridget's RC Primary School, Warrington

Somewhere In The World Today

Somewhere in the world today . . .
A huddle of children are hyperactively debating football
Near the untidy bins.

A cast of radiant hawks squawking endlessly
Across the gloomy, moonlit, sapphire sky.

A clowder of scavenging cats prowling restlessly
Down in the shadowy, deep, dark alley.

A gaggle of hungry geese diving savagely
Down in the gloomy depths of the lake.

Daniel Mahoney (9)
St Bridget's RC Primary School, Warrington

Somewhere In The World Today

Somewhere in the world today . . .
A huddle of calm children are working hard and silently
In the classroom on a small table.

A muster of plump peacocks showing off
their colourful feathers vainly in an immense zoo.

A host of small sparrows
Chirping loudly in a pear tree.

A nest of rabbits scurrying for food
In the tiny pen.

A litter of cute cubs lying in the beautiful daisies
On a hot summer's day.

A kindle of kittens cuddling on the fluffy rug
In front of the fire.

A school of dolphins swimming in and out
Of the deep blue ocean.

A sloth of bad tempered bears
Fighting in the forest noisily and viciously.

Alicia Wright (10)
St Bridget's RC Primary School, Warrington

Somewhere In A School Today

Somewhere in a school today . . .
A group of noiseless children
Gossiping to each other in a windy corner
In the playground.

A huddle of unkind teachers
Whispering angrily
In the light-blue coloured staffroom.

A gang of nasty boys bullying repeatedly
On the way out of the big, green gates.

A draught of sweet little fish swimming rapidly
In a tank in a messy classroom.

A herd of stampeding children
Running out of school
When the clock strikes 3 o'clock.

Alexander Hardy (10)
St Bridget's RC Primary School, Warrington

Somewhere In The World Today

Somewhere in the world today . . .
A group of hyperactive children are messing about
In the classroom.

Somewhere in the world today,
A school of clever dolphins are doing acrobatics sharply
In the see-through ocean.

Somewhere in the world today,
A huddle of spotty geeks are rampaging through a book
In the neat and tidy library.

Natalie Dobbin (10)
St Bridget's RC Primary School, Warrington

Somewhere In The World today

Somewhere in the world today . . .
A table of perplexed children are hesitantly multiplying
Formidable sums on the large, red cushions.

A stampede of eager teachers are insanely bolting
To the staffroom in the long, narrow corridor.

A gang of timid girls are gazing dreamily at a boy
From the corner of the playground.

A room of disobedient boys are assembled
In the towering hall.

Andrew Roe (10)
St Bridget's RC Primary School, Warrington

Somewhere In The World Today

Somewhere in the world today
A sloth of bears carnivorously rampaging through the forest.

Somewhere in the world today
A pod of imperturbable seals silently floating freely in the ocean.

Somewhere in the world today
A flock of falcons squawking over a shred of decaying meat.

Somewhere in the world today
A herd of muscly mammoths fighting for power.

Samuel Mulholland (10)
St Bridget's RC Primary School, Warrington

Somewhere In The World Today

Somewhere in the world today . . .
A huddle of hyperactive children drawing Monet
Quietly on the fresh grass.

A huddle of perfect pupils sketching Monet
In a park blowing a gale.

A litter of growing cubs are investigating gloomily
In the dirty zoo.

A litter of purring kittens are growling nonchalantly
In a smelly basket.

A nest of cute rabbits are searching slowly
In a smelly cage outside.

A litter of slushy pigs are crawling
In muddy water quietly.

A group of detrimental bears
Are hunting barbarically.

Toni Armstrong (9)
St Bridget's RC Primary School, Warrington

Somewhere In The World Today . . .

A group of sensitive children colouring stridently
In the bulky, blue classroom.

A litter of growling puppies racing speedily
Round the dark blue bedroom.

A sloth of hairy bears growling fiercely
In the dark, green forest.

Jordan Sutton (10)
St Bridget's RC Primary School, Warrington

Somewhere In The World Today

Somewhere in the world today . . .
A class of calm children are reading quietly
On the large cushions.
A gaggle of exasperated geese
Are assaulting uproariously on the mean grass.
A nest of cute rabbits, slumbering tranquilly
In a peaceful hutch in the corner.

Louise Mannion (9)
St Bridget's RC Primary School, Warrington

Fly Attack

Mr Chung loved flies, he had a dozen at least,
From the smallest black dots to bluebottle beasts.
A group of small flies laid eggs on his head,
While the other great giants slept in his bed.

He's trained half his flies to do super tricks,
From lobbing some stones to chucking sharp sticks.
In their secret lair they were devising a plan,
They'd start on the army, then take over man.

They loaded their machine guns, the windows were manned,
When the planes came into fire, they'd jump into the sand.
Killing people one by one, the world was getting worried,
From Japan to America, the flies quickly scurried.

They had destroyed America, everyone was vexed,
Flies were spreading everywhere,
What would happen next?

Oliver Morrissey (9) & Connor Irving (10)
St Paul of the Cross RC Primary School, Warrington

Emily Evens - Bat Girl

Emily loves bats, lots of different kinds
Even in school, she wouldn't get them off her mind.

Emily went to bed and what a sight to see
She hung herself upside down like a bat on an old oak tree.

Those hairy bats saw Emily one bright and starry night
They were planning to give Emily a huge and scary fright.

They flung her down the stairs and out of the front door
They brought her to their den and dumped her on the floor.

Those scary bats flew over her with wings like flapping kites
She thought she was seeing stars like she does on stunning nights.

Suddenly those flying bats picked her up and up without a stop
Up to now she didn't have a care.

They took her up to the tallest tree and laid her down to rest
Now she's part of their family, she lives in their little nest.

So if you see a bat, remember not to scream
You could end up like Emily and fulfill your every dream.

Danielle Drinkel & Laura Cawley (10)
St Paul of the Cross RC Primary School, Warrington

The Watchers

'What's that?' said the old man with his sword at the ready
and the clock struck midnight as the hands stood steady.

Green eyes lit up across the house
nothing stirred, not even a mouse.

Fear jabbed at his insides like needles as he shouted
'What's that?'

But no one answered his echoing call
as the silence surged softly back through the empty hall.

At the edge of the forest remained the two glowing eyes
as the old man turned back into the house, he could hear their
muffled cries.

As the darkness surged softly back to cover the blackness of
the night
the man closed the door and the eyes went out of sight.

Alex Gordon & Michael Rafferty (10)
St Paul of the Cross RC Primary School, Warrington

The Phantom Watchers

'Please, anybody, open the door,' wailed the weak and helpless boy
standing outside
As the clouds grew deeper and darker, livid and irate.
But no one answered to his resonant knock
Apart from the ticking of the indistinct clock.
As the obscure but dim shadows crept silently across the floor
The grimy little rats sped briskly through the open door.
But only the faint murmur of the small boy could be heard
As the trees rustled silently and a wise owl stared
At that lonely, nebulous figure standing all alone.
'Who's there?' whispered the small boy
But all that answered was a raucous moan.
He turned away slowly, head bowed down
As he plodded back puzzled, with a great, substantial frown.

Laura Wynne & Michael Pearce (10)
St Paul of the Cross RC Primary School, Warrington

The Heard But Not Seen

'Who's there?' asked the weary traveller
Looking for a source of light,
And he banged on the old oak door,
Knocking with all his might.
As the clouds grew dark
And dense above his head,
He gazed through the misty windows,
'Who's there?' he said.

But no one answered his solitary call
As he stood on the step alone and forlorn,
His head hung low,
His eyes cast down,
Inside, his heart was torn.

Only a host of phantom specters
Heard the traveller's cry,
As he turned around slowly,
He heaved a very heavy sigh.

Sam O'Garra & Claire Scott (10)
St Paul of the Cross RC Primary School, Warrington

Boring Beth - Spider-Woman

Beth loved spiders, she had a million at least
They climbed up to her window and back down for the feast.

Every time Beth went to sleep they climbed up to her bed
Even in the morning light they span a little web.

All over the bed covers a silver thread was spun
Every time her mum came in they knew that battle had begun.

Her mum was armed with a duster, a big old feathery thing
When battle began Beth brought out the big old spider king.

He began to march his army like war had just begun
Pulling up her skirt, she began to scream and run.

Lucy Smith (10) & Laura Cooke-Jones (9)
St Paul of the Cross RC Primary School, Warrington

My Family Are All Animals

My family are all animals:
My mum's a chimpanzee,
My nana's just like a panda
And my grandad's a busy bee.

My dad's a kangaroo
And my brothers are big fat roos.
But as for me, I'm so, so cool,
So I must be a sleek, slim mule!

Zachary Later (10)
Styal CP School

Cats

Staring, staring
Are the cat's big, round eyes
As they look round uncaring.

Prowling, prowling
His flexible, sleek body
Spoilt by his scowling.

Faster, faster
Are his steps to catch his prey
To take home to his master.

They say he's an alley cat
Who prowls around his patch.
Stalking and walking throughout the night
He catches his prey
And eats him up in one big bite.
Then he turns and heads off home
Through tunnels and passages
After his long, big roam.

I wonder, I wonder
As in my bed I am sat
Is he really a bad cat
Who attacks you
When you go near?
Or does he sit with his owner
Who has looked after him year after year?

Katie Halliwell (10)
Styal CP School

A Boy Called Bill

This boy called Bill
Caught a chill.
He had the wheezes
And a nose that sneezes.
That boy called Bill
Is always ill.

Molly Finnigan (9)
Styal CP School

The Story Of Charlie Who Ate Too Much

Charlie was both slim and fit
He never overate a bit
His mother proudly people told
'One day my Charlie will win gold'
But Charlie was tired of being good
And eating everything he should
So when his mother wasn't looking
He scoffed the cakes she had been cooking
And then he ate up all his tea
And even sweets she did not see.

At school the foolish boy began
To walk whereas before he ran
He now began to sit at table
And eat as much as he was able
And eating cake in class was caught
And because of all the sweets he'd bought
No longer was he good at sport.

Now daily Charlie grew bigger and bigger
He no longer had an athlete's figure
His mother cried out in despair
'I try to stop him, it's just not fair
He's eating sweets and drinking Coke
His healthy diet is now a joke
And every sensible rule he's broke.'

When Sports Day came, the fat little lad
Was feeling terribly bad
And now instead of coming first
Poor Charlie, *burst!*

Tim Marshall (11)
Styal CP School

My Mum And Dad Are Vampires

My mum and dad are vampires,
Our landlord is a ghost,
For tea he eats fried chicken,
For lunch he eats burnt toast.

My nanny she's a zombie,
She haunts me in my room,
But I think she's better in Egypt,
In that filthy haunted tomb.

My grandad he's a yeti,
He likes to live in snow,
But I think he's the weirdest,
Because he ate all my dough.

Me, I'm just a werewolf,
With white fangs and sharp claws,
I could eat all my relatives,
In my large, wide jaws.

Madeleine Smith (9)
Styal CP School

My Limerick

There was a young schoolboy called Pete,
Who stuck coloured pens on his feet,
Now wherever he goes
And he wriggles his toes,
He can draw on the ground,
    Now that's neat!

Jack Holmes (9)
Styal CP School

Kennings

A sly creeper
A bounding leaper

A slow strutter
A wild nutter

A stripy thing
A furry thing.

A catalogue to make me a tiger! *Raaa!*

Nina Lynch (9)
Styal CP School

Greedy Dog

I sat in the kennel and nibbled my food
There lay down beside me a dog in a mood
Who barked as he pushed me into the wall
'Your problem my son, is your belly's too small
Your legs are too thin, take a lesson from me
I may be a bulldog but I'm nice, you'll agree
And I've lasted some dog years by playing this hunch:
The larger the packet, the bigger the munch!

The bigger the munch, then the huger the dog
The deeper the water, the more to hog
You'll always be thin, with just a small tin
You really don't want to be as thin as a cat
Just like me, you want to be fat.'

Ollie Bayne (11)
Styal CP School

A Person

A food needer
A big feeder

A thing that has rights
A thing that will still fight

A thing that needs air
A thing that wants care

A catalogue to make me a . . .
Person!

Rio Tuli (9)
Styal CP School

The Young Man From Peru

There was a young man from Peru,
Who got a job in the zoo.
He fed all the parrots,
With onions and carrots,
When asked why said,
'I ain't got a clue.'

Emily Talbot (8)
Styal CP School

Kenning

A yellow dot
A pale spot

A leaf muncher
A crawly gunger

A flower sucker
A beautiful looker

A catalogue to make me a butterfly.

Eleanor Jackson (9)
Styal CP School

Brothers I Have Got

Of all the brothers I have got
Here are a few I have not forgot.
Brother Sam likes ham and jam
While brother Ollie likes a strawberry lolly.
Brother Tim is clever and slim
While brother Matt is silly and fat.
Brother Zach's a pain in the back
While brother Jay keeps out of the way.
Brother Josh eats a lot of nosh
While brother Tibbles just has a nibble.
Brother Phil wins twelve nil
While brother Paul can't score at all.
Brother Trevor is always clever
While brother Cupid is very stupid.
Brother Blair has got no hair
While brother Daniel looks like a spaniel.
But the weirdest brother I have got
Is very small and eats a lot.
He's helpful and kind and his name is Bert
He won't wear trousers - only a skirt!

Joanna Hyde (10)
Styal CP School

St Mary's Church

Dark gods whispering in my ear, scratching at the edge,
driving me mad.

The hall from aeons ago, the sight of generations past.
The haunting spirits in my mind, trying to bend reality.

The dead bodies taunting my tastebuds,
The grimy taste of death on wings.

The touch of time long gone,

The ghosts' hearts vibrating in my ear,
Throbbing on the edge of sound.

> When once I was nervous,
> Now I am terrified!

Hatham Rahman (11)
Warren Wood Primary School

St Mary's Church

The organ is dull,
Like the howl of a bull,
Thundering,
Like the commands of the gods,
Dark and gloomy,
Like the empty underworld,
Quiet,
The forgotten land,
I can taste the anger of the souls cursed eternally to their grave,
I can feel the beautifully carved wood as soft as silk,
I can smell the unsettled dust drifting in the air,
It makes me feel alone in the dark,
Empty.

Alex Ellis (10)
Warren Wood Primary School

St Mary's Church

The organ,
Mystical creatures of evil,
Escaping, breaking out never to return.

I see the lion head,
Escaping from its imprisonment.

Taste of age, battling on my tongue.

The smell of death,
Escaping from the grave,
Fighting, fighting for freedom.

Feeling the spirits clamping me to my very seat,
Locked in a world of life and death . . .
Depression overwhelms them,
Knowing that one day they too will perish in the fires of hell.
Feeling the cold air touch my skin,
The power of evil is breaking out,
The blackness touches me,
Showing its true power,
For destruction is close at hand,
The apocalypse draws near.

Christopher Cooney (11)
Warren Wood Primary School

St Mary's Church

The organ like the roaring of an ocean,
Stands tall like a soldier.
The rainbow of a dream,
Reflected colours dancing on the floor,
The taste of dust from years ago.
Memories of lives lived,
The touch of smooth, varnished wood,
Like silk on a best dress.
The smell of fresh air,
Touching my nose,
The feeling of warmth and care,
Surrounding me.

Katie Hicklin (11)
Warren Wood Primary School

St Mary's Church

The organ dark and mysterious,
Like the demon was rising from the underground.
The Warren Wood crest blue and gold,
Blue as the water surrounding me,
Gold as the morning sun, like the gladiator's shield.
The taste of the salt dust.
I can feel the smoothness of the varnish.

Alice Ashurst (11)
Warren Wood Primary School

St Mary's Church

The organ as deep as the ocean,
Like waves crashing against rocks.
The taste of wooden seats and wooden floors,
Creaking and cracking as we walk.
Colourful windows with beautiful pictures,
As bright as the sun and as colourful as a rainbow.
The olden day wood rotting away into thin air.
The smell of sandstone from hundreds of years ago.
It makes me feel happy.

Rebecca Gill (10)
Warren Wood Primary School

St Mary's Church

The organ bellowing in my ear,
Like the Man U derby has just kicked off.

I see the glazed windows,
As colourful as the rainbow,
Seeing the past of Jesus' life.

The graves lying there,
Cold, wet, dark, but we know
They have gone to a better place.

I feel the wood, going back in time,
On a bench, feeling sorry for myself.

The smell of dust,
Being there 700 years,
People coughing from the dead.

Andrew Scott (11)
Warren Wood Primary School

St Mary's Church

The deep, undamaged, delightful reverberation of the organ.
The fancy imitation of the coloured stained glass.
The mouthful of particles from years back.
I feel like both of my grandpas are supervising me.
I can feel the hard, dry, inflexible wood.

Adam Archer (10)
Warren Wood Primary School

St Mary's Church

The organ as loud as a howling werewolf,
Loud, deep voices,
Through the keys it is played,
Rows of pews all in perfect lines with
Magnificent carvings around them.
Stained glass windows,
As bright as the sun gleaming through them.
Ancient dust wafting in and out of gaps,
Floating through the air, making different tastes.
The feel of wood and sandstone bricks,
As hard as iron surrounding you in the church.
The smell of air that has been smelt many times before
Wafting gently around the church.
Feeling holy and amazed at the objects in the church.

Sam Woodall (10)
Warren Wood Primary School

St Mary's Church

The mighty, black organ,
A volcano erupting with deep, dark notes,
The sun shining through the glorious windows
Covered in colours,
A glass version of God.
I can taste the old, battered wood right next to me.
I can feel the old but strong patterned wood on my cheek
And a soft cushion on my feet
As it springs up when I lift my feet.
I can smell the fresh, clean air and the smell of wood,
Yet another gift from God.
This church makes me thank God for His magnificent gifts.

Nicole Bramhall (10)
Warren Wood Primary School

St Mary's Church

The organ,
Like a loud, lurking lion.
Your vision,
Vaguely scanning the huge church around you.
The taste of recent years,
Of howling happiness that has now passed by.
Feel the old wood material,
Carved like an eagle's feathers.
Smell the shivering, dusty veins of the church.
Feel the fluttering feelings that have passed through this church.

Ben Hackney (10)
Warren Wood Primary School

St Mary's Church

The organ, roaring like an angry,
Fiery, fuming, furious rhino.

The angel in the corner,
Glowing like the global, fiery sun.

I can taste ashes burning my mouth,
The ashes from years ago.

I can feel the sponge on the old, ragged seats,
As soft as a fur coat.

I can smell the wood chippings
From the old, ragged chairs.

It makes me feel upset
For all the people who have died.

Dean Hemmings (10)
Warren Wood Primary School

St Mary's Church

The organ, like a furious lion roaring,
Getting ready to catch its prey.
The pulpit, bright with brown windows,
Glowing in the light.
God making sure the church is bright.
I can taste the wood, old and dusty,
Carved into beautiful patterns.
I can feel the old planks of wood,
Cold under my feet.
I can smell crisp, clear varnish
From the pews.
It makes me feel like dark gods
Are following me everywhere.
I'm a part of Heaven.

Kate Kenyon (10)
Warren Wood Primary School

St Mary's Church

The organ, like a bull bellowing, in a bull's field.
The window, colourful and bright and beautiful in the room.
The dust, as small as a mouse in a cage.
The lovely hand made from wood, hundreds and hundreds of
years ago.
The smell of the stone in the church.
I think of all the dead people in the world and in my family.

Billy Lomax (10)
Warren Wood Primary School

St Mary's Church

The organ, like a thunderstorm,
Reverend Schoone's voice chattering away,
I can taste the wooden pews,
The strange taste of dust in my mouth,
The comfort of the cushion on my knees,
I can feel the Holy Spirit,
The smell of clean wood on the pews and panels,
It smells new in the heritage centre,
It makes me feel special,
It makes me feel happy and sad at the same time.

Matthew Southam (11)
Warren Wood Primary School

Seven Ages Of Man

(Based on a passage from Shakespeare's 'As You Like It')

All the world's a stage,
And all the men and women merely players.
They have their exits and entrances,
His acts being seven ages.
First the infant, reluctant and repulsive,
Whining for better things in life.
Next the schoolboy, trying to hold onto old ways
With a face redder than the sun walking with anger's blight.
The third age is a teenager, ungrateful and disturbing,
Thinking they have no responsibility except to be free.
And then the young man as hard working as an ant,
Trying harder.
Then swiftly the middle-aged head teacher,
Wise in the arts of intelligence.
Then the sixth age looms,
It is unwelcome as his hair shows this.
Then senility,
Losing teeth and other senses.
As they perish,
May they live a better life after death.

Lewis Wilkes (10)
Warren Wood Primary School

The Seven Ages Of Man

(Based on a passage from Shakespeare's 'As You Like It')]

All the world's a stage,
And all the men and women are merely players.
They have their exits and their entrances,
And one man in his time plays many parts,
His acts being the seven ages.
First the infant, miniature and chubby,
Choking and wailing for nurse's attention.
Next the schoolboy, shouting and being rude,
Taking as long as he can, dragging his bag along the stony floor.
The third age is a teenager dumped on the sofa,
Hanging around the park, vandalism on his mind.
And then the young man, as strong as a bird,
Running to the gym to work out again!
Then comes the middle-aged head teacher,
Whose stomach is as large as a beach ball,
Living on food, food, nothing but food.
The sixth age is brittle-boned but loved,
A man living the rest of his life in a lovely holiday home.
Last comes senility, nothing working,
More death than life in the body.
He exits now,
He rots away . . .
Only death awaits him.

Hannah Griffiths (10)
Warren Wood Primary School

Seven Ages Of Man

(Based on a passage from Shakespeare's 'As You Like It')

All the world's a stage,
And all the men and women merely players,
They have their exits and entrances
And one man in his time plays many parts,
His acts being seven ages.
First, the young infant, dependent and helpless,
The little seed of a new generation.
Next, the schoolboy, reluctant to work,
Bored face, walking slowly to school on those days.
The third stage is a teenager, carefree and soppy,
Jumping in loving delight,
And then the young man, as funny as a comedian,
Joking on stage.
Then the middle-aged headmaster,
Full of responsibility.
The sixth age of man is old and white-haired,
Sitting in his chair.
Then last comes senility, losing his senses,
Life is over.

Rida Fatima (11)
Warren Wood Primary School

Seven Ages Of Man

(Based on a passage from Shakespeare's 'As You Like It')

All the world's a stage,
And all the men and women merely players,
They have their exits and entrances
And one man in his time plays many parts,
His acts being seven ages.
First the infant, helpless and harmless,
But then again always crying noisily and disturbingly
for his mother.
Next the schoolboy, whining and frowning,
Eyes gazing at the floor,
Like a cat watching and waiting for prey.
The third age is a teenager, loveable and soppy,
Hand in hand with his lover.
And then the young man, as fit as a plank of wood,
Working out and helping others.
Then comes the middle-aged head teacher,
With a bearded face and rounded tummy.
The sixth age of man is skinny,
Retired and spending time with his family.
Then last comes senility, sans senses, sans everything.
    The show has nearly ended.

Sophie Burton (11)
Warren Wood Primary School

The Seven Ages Of Man

(Based on a passage from Shakespeare's 'As You Like It')

All the world's a stage,
And all the men and women merely players.
They have their exits and their entrances,
And one man in his time plays many parts,
His acts being seven ages.
First the infant, moaning and groaning,
Screaming and whining for adoption.
Next the schoolboy, tired and bored,
Thunder-shocked eyes, dawdling and lonely.
The third age is a teenager, snappy and sulky,
Dumped by his girlfriend, his eyes big and bulky.
And then the young man, as clever as a teacher,
Teaching pupils all day, happy and joyful.
Then comes the middle-aged head teacher,
Chubby and bulky with no hair at all.
The sixth age of man is old and wise,
Spending his days keeping fit.
Then last comes senility, without senses.
A virtual loss for relatives and friends.

Josh Hargreaves (11)
Warren Wood Primary School

The Seven Ages Of Man

(Based on a passage from Shakespeare's 'As You Like It')

All the world's a stage and all the men and women merely players.
They have their exits and their entrances,
And one man in his time plays many parts,
His acts being seven ages.
First the infant, cute and cheeky,
Crying and wriggling, wanting his mother.
Next the schoolboy, moaning and stressful, angry-faced,
Drooping like a slow snail.
The third age of man is a teenager,
Muddy and grumpy,
Non-stop listening to music, playing on the computer lazily.
And then the young man, as clever as an accountant,
Working on his laptop and going to smart meetings.
Then comes the middle-aged head teacher,
Rounder than a rhino's belly.
The sixth age of man is old and wise
And always there when you need them,
Playing golf on the green grass to keep them healthy,
To keep them going.
Then last comes senility, lost eyesight, almost rotted away.

Chelsea Hill (10)
Warren Wood Primary School

The Seven Ages Of Man

(Based on a passage from Shakespeare's 'As You Like It')

All the world's a stage,
And all the men and women merely players.
They have their exits and entrances,
And one man in his time plays many parts,
His acts being seven ages.
First the infant, looking and staring,
Next the young schoolboy clean as clean,
Carrying his school bag happily.
The third age is the lover, teenager,
Stompy and stormy,
But big and sloppy to his girlfriends.
And then the young man,
As fit as a fish,
Showing off to his girlfriends.
Then comes the middle-aged head teacher,
Round as round, but a very good dad.
The sixth age of man is old and wise,
Spending his days gardening.
Then comes senility,
Close to death,
He reaches the exit.

Megan Kenyon (10)
Warren Wood Primary School

Seven Ages Of Man

(Based on a passage from Shakespeare's 'As You Like It')

All the world's a stage,
All the men and women merely players.
They have their exits and entrances
And one man in his time plays many parts,
His acts being the seven ages.
First the infant, sweet and smiley,
Innocently giggling and shrieking with laughter in the nurse's arms.
Next the schoolboy, whining but clever,
Frowning face with muddy marks,
Trudging like a snail on his way.
Next the third age, the teenager, moody and stroppy,
No girlfriend in sight,
Jobless, moody and bored.
And then the young man, working as hard as a beaver,
Earning a useful wage.
Then comes the middle-aged head teacher,
Plump and roundish, settled down happily with a family.
The sixth age of man is old and wise,
Telling his lifelong tales.
And last comes senility, frail and dependent.
Then he leaves his body, *sans everything.*

Rhea Kay (10)
Warren Wood Primary School

Seven Ages Of Man

(Based on a passage from Shakespeare's 'As You Like It')

All the world's a stage
And all the men and women merely players.
They have their entrances and exits
And one man in his time plays many parts,
His acts being seven ages.
First the infant, rosy cheeks and chubby,
Whining and bawling for mother's help.
Next the schoolboy, moaning, 'Why me?'
Stamping his feet.
The third age is a teenager, sly and a liar.
Then the young man, smarter than a bank manager
On his broken PC.
Then the middle-aged head teacher,
Rounder than a hippo.
Then comes the sixth age,
He spends his time working.
Last comes senility, hunchbacked.
Doom is on its way.
Maybe it will be a good thing.

Liam Bockelmann (10)
Warren Wood Primary School

The Seven Ages Of Man

(Based on a passage from Shakespeare's 'As You Like It')

All the world's a stage,
And all the men and women merely players.
They have their exits and their entrances
And one man in his time plays many parts,
His acts being the seven ages.
First the infant,
Whining and screaming in the nurse's arms.
Next the schoolboy, moaning and whining,
Scruffy and tatty,
Creeping like a spider with a crooked, hunched back.
The third age is a teenager,
Annoyingly moody all the time,
Whining and crying at night because he has no lover.
Next comes the young man, his duty to be a soldier
And he fights with honour, trying to be the best of them all.
Then comes the middle-aged head teacher,
With a big, round belly,
His responsibility is high.
The sixth age of man is a knobbly-kneed old man,
With his crooked white hair,
As white as skeletal bones.
Then last comes senility,
Looking like the walking dead,
For all his senses have gone and then he goes . . .
To a better place.

Carl Bownas (10)
Warren Wood Primary School

Seven Ages Of Man

(Based on a passage from Shakespeare's 'As You Like It')

All the world's a stage
And all the men and women merely players.
They have their exits and their entrances
And one man in his time plays many parts,
His acts being seven ages.
First the infant, chubby and sweet,
Crying for mother's help.
Next the schoolboy, teary and banging his rock-hard conkers
on the ground,
Singing on his way to school.
The third age is a teenager,
Singing and sharing his love,
Happy under the magical, bright, shiny apple tree.
And then the young man,
As smart as a teacher, as strict as anything.
Then comes the middle-aged head teacher,
Rounder than a football.
The sixth age of man is old, bald,
Spending his boring time playing bingo.
Then last comes senility,
The life cycle starts all over again.

Jessica Bajic (11)
Warren Wood Primary School

The Seven Ages Of Man

(Based on a passage from Shakespeare's 'As You Like It')

All the world's a stage
And all the men and women merely players.
They have their exits and entrances
And one man in his time plays many parts,
His acts being seven ages.
First the infant, calm and cheeky,
Coughing hazardously, desperate for a gentle mother's hand.
Next the schoolboy, trudging along the road that is hell,
Long face and curled lip,
Muttering and kicking quietly
As the branches creak under squirming feet.
The third age is the teenager,
Grouchy and cruel,
Constantly prodding buttons on mobile phones.
And then the young man, as optimistic as an actor,
Zooming down the road, looking for a job to fulfill his dream.
Then comes the middle-aged head teacher,
Rounder than the world as he relaxes in his weary office.
The sixth age of man is bald,
Loving and forgiving,
Always having time for grandchildren.
Last comes senility,
The seventh deadly age, practically dead,
Somnolent and weak, wasting away to nothing.

Laura Matthews (11)
Warren Wood Primary School

St Mary's Church

The organ roaring like a tiger chasing its prey.
Stained glass windows reflecting God's light.
The taste of dust floating round the church blowing in my face.
I can feel God's love wrapping round me.
I can smell wood from years ago.
I can feel God reaching inside me.

Joshua Bradshaw (10)
Warren Wood Primary School

Seven Ages Of Man

(Based on a passage from Shakespeare's 'As You Like It')

All the world's a stage
And all the men and women merely players.
They have their exits and entrances
And one man in his time plays many parts,
His acts being seven ages.
First the infant small and annoying,
Screeching and moaning all day long.
Next a schoolboy moaning and bored,
A sick face and slowly plodding along.
The third stage is a teenager thinking he's cool and smart,
Messing about with his mates.
And then the young man in the gym all day long.
Then comes the middle aged headmaster round as a rhino
And as old as a turtle.
The sixth age of man wrinkly and old but you still love them.
Then comes the blind, deaf, no teeth, can't remember anything
Stage, close to death.

John Kay (11)
Warren Wood Primary School

Winter

It's very chilly,
You'd better put warm clothes on
Or the cold might bite.

The warm, cosy fire,
I am roasting my cold feet,
Whilst eating hot toast.

Crunching through the snow,
Robins tweeting by my side,
Singing as I go.

Ella Williams (7)
Wilmslow Preparatory School

Winter Days

The glum, white, bare trees,
The drab, miserable colours
And the cool, chilly wind.

The frosty, cool air,
The bitter taste of winter
And the icy snowflakes.

The icicles hanging,
The cold, white coat of winter
And the gusty wind.

Amber Saleem (8)
Wilmslow Preparatory School

Winter

The glum, white, bare trees,
Robins tweeting by your side,
Strong winds blow in your face.

The cosy, warm fire,
Snuggle up in bed
With a hot water bottle.

Crunching through the snow,
When the snow falls so softly,
Like pretty snowdrops.

Celyn Wynn Griffiths (7)
Wilmslow Preparatory School

Ruthless Dragons

The dragon is vile,
The dragon is sly,
With a forked tongue
And glittering eyes.

He spits smoke,
With glowing breath,
He has fang-like teeth
And oily scales.

His muscles move sinuously,
His voice is sinister,
He is awesome and deceitful,
Powerful and wicked.

He is cold-blooded,
Greedy and rich,
Devours princesses,
He's wild and untamed.

His cold, blue eyes,
Rip into your skin,
With his green silk wings,
He flies silently.

He looks indestructible,
Vicious and gargantuan,
With his lizard-like face
And monster-like jaws.

ManiMekala Fuller (9)
Wilmslow Preparatory School

The Vicious Dragon

Roaring like a lion, the dragon shakes the ground
As it leaps down the street
With its frightening sounds.

With its leathery wings,
Its horns like jewels owned by a king,
Its mouth dripping with blood.

With its rough, knobbly scales,
A flashing, thumping tail,
It pounds along the deserted town.

It moves like a tornado, looking for food,
Its mouth puffing with fire,
Its fangs dripping with blood.

Katherine Gardner   (9)
Wilmslow Preparatory School

Winter

It was a cold and frosty morning.
I watched everyone making snow angels.
The ice was sparkling and children made snowmen.
The trees were bare,
Some children were swinging on the low branches
And falling into the snow,
Which covered the whole of their bodies.

Everyone went inside
And watched the weather forecast.
It said the snow would melt.
They all went outside again and ice skated.
They had a good time before it went.
I listened to the robins singing.
They were sort of saying,
'Join in before it goes.'
So that's what I did.

Olivia Norton (9)
Wilmslow Preparatory School

Winter

See the snow falling from the sky,
Slowly forming a carpet.
The snowflakes twirling through the mist,
Down into the icy sea of snow.

The little robin pecks at the snow,
No worms to be seen it thought he.
And through the fog a figure came,
To clear away the white mush
Lying on the bird table.

The sound of laughter is to be heard,
As children sled down the hill.
Snowmen are being built all over the place,
There'll be no snow left soon.

As I feared, the snow disappeared,
No whiteness to be seen.
The sun came out and invited the spring,
We'll have to wait till next year.

Sophie Feather (10)
Wilmslow Preparatory School

The Hockey Match

Walking to the pitch,
Getting ready for the ball,
Different people,
Anticipation and nerves,
Ready to play and waiting.

The loud whistle goes,
I run forward and tackle,
Everything is tense,
Crowd is shouting and jumping,
Ball is pushed from side to side.

Someone hits the ball,
Ball rolls down the rocky pitch,
Goalkeeper misses,
We wipe the sweat off our heads,
We have definitely won.

Referee decides,
The air is spooky and tense,
Everything quiet,
My heart thumping in my chest,
Wind starts to blow and rain falls.

We are now waiting,
We are not sure what to do,
The crowd shout wildly,
Referee blows his whistle,
It is 1-0, we have won.

We walk off the pitch,
In triumph we shout, Hooray,'
Nerves have gone quickly,
We have a drink and biscuit,
We have achieved our great goal!

Olivia Hill (11)
Wilmslow Preparatory School

The Race

My heart was beating,
The crowd was cheering madly,
I heard the gun shoot,
I leapt back in the water,
I felt like a cube of ice.

Arms like water wheels,
I hurtled through the water,
Everything vanished,
Fountain of water sprayed me,
Hard to breathe, so gasped for breath.

The end was so near,
The tension was building fast,
Could I arrive first?
Could I hit the wall to stop the clock?
Finished the race. Great, I had won!

Gabby Westington (11)
Wilmslow Preparatory School

The Match Of Guilt

Five minutes to go,
Tension is building slowly,
Walking to the pitch,
The opposition staring,
Feet like jelly, hands shaking.

5, 4, 3, 2, 1,
Go, go go! Running, jumping,
Shouting, 'Pass the ball,'
Shoot, shoot, score 1-0 to us,
Nerves going, keenness building.

Legs not like jelly,
Referee blows the whistle,
'Next quarter please now,'
The smell of winning is near,
Go, run, jump, land, shoot, *shoot, score.*

No! The score is 1-1,
We are now like hungry wolves,
Waiting for our prey,
The ball is now a bullet,
Waiting to fire in the net.

Penalty to us,
Smell of victory is far,
The score is 2-1 to them,
We are no longer happy,
We walk off the pitch heads down!

Cerys Owen
Wilmslow Preparatory School

The Top Board

The water is still,
Nerves take over my body,
My hands are shaking
As I walk to the ladder,
Time appears to have slowed down.

My body is numb,
I slowly climb the ladder,
The crowd falls silent,
I drown in a sea of nerves,
I am at the top, looking down.

The crowd starts to cheer,
I face the board and run fast,
I am in the air,
I pierce the water's surface,
A very successful dive!

Jennifer Fishbourne (11)
Wilmslow Preparatory School

The Sea

The clear sea glistens,
The gentle waves lap the shore,
How peaceful it is.
The cool sea reflects the sun,
Wonderful, peaceful, turquoise.

The young fish darting,
Oblivious to humans,
Colourful, graceful.
The sea protects all fish,
Fish are happy in the sea.

Snorklers swimming around,
A brave snorkler disturbs the peace,
Fish dart away.
They are terrified of us,
Everyone is happy here.

Rachael Killworth (11)
Wilmslow Preparatory School

Netball Match

Shouting, jumping, tense,
Nerves rushing, ball side to side,
Watching to score goals,
Running, tension rising fast,
People watching constantly.

Reaching the goalpost,
Shooting, cheering, excited,
Waiting to win soon,
Having a break, ready to start,
Everyone shouting, 'Come on!'

Throwing, catching, mark,
Last quarter, ready to score,
Girls pushing, waiting,
The temptation to win now,
Eyes on the ball as it moves.

Winning, winning, won,
Everyone pleased and happy,
Other team upset,
Celebrating together,
Enjoying the victory.

Victoria Rossetti
Wilmslow Preparatory School

Weather

The fog is so thick,
Gloominess hangs in the air,
I feel I'm alone,
The wind whistles in my ears,
When fog comes, I'm sad and scared.

The sun is so hot,
The rays hit my skin warmly,
Feet hurt in the sun,
My skin must not burn, but tan,
The sun, a ball of fire.

The rain is so sad,
The spirits could be crying,
Maybe they're weeping,
Rain cannot make you happy,
All rain is . . . lots of tears.

The snow is so deep,
Like gems it shines in the sun,
Too cold for fingers,
You might think of it as ice cream,
Snow, my winter wonderland.

Phoebe Broome (10)
Wilmslow Preparatory School

Sad Days And Happy Days

Sad days, happy days.
What memories do you have?
Are they of the sea,
Roaring, crashing and hissing,
Like an angry, fierce lion?

Sad days, happy days.
What memories do you have?
Are they of the sky,
White, fluffy clouds above you,
Like marshmallows, soft and light?

Sad days, happy days.
What memories do you have?
Are they of flowers?
No! They're of my grandma gone,
Gone forever, up above.

She left me, alone,
Now I'm on my own, alone.
The grass is still green,
Even though Grandma's left me.

Sad days, happy days.
What memories do you have?
Mostly happy, but,
One sad one, of my grandma, gone!

Katarina Holt (11)
Wilmslow Preparatory School